T0365871

Le Docteur et l'ane
AL5972 A.D 1972
R.C. Hughes Artificer

This handsome carving of the Docteur et l'ane
was presented to Dr. Alfred Tuttle by the artificer,
as a gift from a grateful patient, among the first
to hear what had happened to his doctor that
very morning. He damn near fell off the table!

To order additional copies of this book, contact:
Xlibris
844-714-8691
www.Xlibris.com
Orders@Xlibris.com

ISBN: Softcover   978-1-4010-9569-7

Library of Congress Control Number: 2003090866

Print information available on the last page

Rev. date: 01/07/2025

TABLE OF CONTENTS

~Preface~

Around the late 1990s, my father began to write his memoirs. At first he was doing it the old way with pencil and paper. But being a physician, he wrote in a script that no one could read. Then he tried transcribing his scribbles using an electric typewriter. But old age had finally taken away the steadiness of the surgeon's hand. So instead of "the" he would get "ttheeeeee." Then my sister Lucy gave him a computer with a word processing program. After that there was no stopping him.

Being blessed with a long life and good memory, the stories just kept coming, and the pages added up. Stories of his youth, his pranks and wisdom learned, were soon followed in no particular order by stories of high school, college, medical school, the War years, and the raising of us kids.

What follows is a collection of these stories, organized into three separate volumes. Volume I primarily contains stories of my father's youth. Volume II are stories of his adult life. And Volume III is dedicated to his experience as a frontline Army physician in Company A of the Twenty-fourth Medical Battalion of the Twenty-fourth Division during World War II in the Pacific Theater.

How he and my mother endured it all I will never know. But somehow I think it has something to do with their ability to see the humor in the twists, turns, and tricks that life plays on us, as well as their ability to spin it into a yarn that all could enjoy. We hope you enjoy these tales of a time gone by, of mischief making and the company of friends, and of the good memories that sweeten life.

Alfred Edward Tuttle, Dr. Al's son

~Acknowledgments~

A number of my friends, neighbors, and family encouraged and helped me in many ways to keep writing little remembrances of my living experiences from the beginning of my birth in a log cabin on the banks of the Allegheny River to the present. I want to thank every one of them:

Mrs. Susan Givens, who is my brother Heath's first born, married to Douglas and is now living on Wiggins Street in Gambier, Ohio, with two children. Jane Tuttle Roester, in Bozeman, Montana, second born. David and Cindy Gompert, third born, living in Alexandria, Virginia, with two children.

Susan Meadowcroft, friend of my daughters, who edited the first few pages in a most professional way showing me where to expand and get the how, when, and where to set the atmosphere. Susan made me realize how different writing a family story is from just telling it to family and close friends. It ordinarily takes only the name of a person, the name of a place and the simple words "*REMEMBER WHEN*" to set the scene as to time, place, and atmosphere. To write the same story of the family remembrances, however, requires a conjuration of glorifying adjectives, verbs, etc., to impact the reader with a word panorama picture.

Mary Florence Sprague, my sister, who was the first to transcribe into readable type the first of my scribbly handwriting.

Mrs. George Pratt, Marian, my next-door neighbor at Longwood at Oakmont, who made meaningful corrections to my spelling without embarrassment to my life long weakness.

 Lucy Tuttle Smith, my youngest daughter who gave to us the most wonderful grandchildren, Alfred Jack, A.J. for short, and Penelope, who will forever be Penny. Lucy gave me the greatest reason for writing most of these remembrances for A.J. and Penny, and their children.

Cindy Mosqueda, the transcriber at Shadyside Hospital, who on her own precious time, put the finishing touches onto a computer disk.

Heath Tuttle, my elder brother, now deceased, who was a traveling sales representative for many years, a local politician, who upon returning each weekend from his travels would dispense the latest jokes, clean, dirty or political. None of which were original, because the ancient Greeks themselves did it, rolling out of their seats laughing in the amphitheater.

Alfred Edward, my son, who matured around us, giving us strength and good humor in support of each of our adventures. I know, he thinks I'm demented at times. That is why he is such a great help to me.

~Dedication~

To my dear wife Louise, I dedicate this collection of remembrances. Louise gave me three wonderful children of whom we are very proud. Louise kept the lid on an immaculate home in spite of the intrusions of mice, rabbits, squirrels, cats, dogs, birds, goldfish, a donkey, and two horses into our home.

Some said that if we had a pig it would have been in the parlor, just to prove that you do not have to be Irish to do so[1].

Louise has always been a gracious host to all friends and neighbors.

Louise never failed to laugh at my lousy jokes and stories no matter how often told.

What a lover too. I often wonder how she put up with me!

1 >From the line in the old tune, "They kept a pig in the parlor."

All About Myself

Where I was born. The log cabin as it stands on April 28, 2003, along the Allegheny River in Godfrey, Pennsylvania.

In the beginning, so I am told, 90-some years ago, on September 28, 1909 at 5 A.M., a young man was seen running on the Pennsylvania railroad track between the rails from Godfrey to White Rock, a small coal mine village, on the south side of the Allegheny River and thirty miles upriver from Pittsburgh, Pennsylvania. He was in a mad dash, hell bent to fetch the coal mine doctor. The doctor's name was Snyder and he had just finished interning at West Penn Hospital. This was his first home delivery for which he would be paid, if he were lucky.

The doctor and this young man jumped into the doctor's buggy and at full gallop on the railroad ties, they went rattling and banging toward Godfrey shouting "DAMN THE TRAINS –FULL SPEED AHEAD."

There, just before the station shed, they bounced off the track onto the lane toward the river and the log cabin where they slid to a stop in a cloud of dust and sweat.

They arrived just in time for the arrival of an infant boy. He already had an older brother, Heath, and sister, Helen. So, from then on the new boy in the house was called Brother.

Remembering conjures the fantasy and joy of returning there barefoot to feel the soft earth, to breathe the fragrances in the breeze; to see the lush green world on this side of the river and way over on the other side of the river where the wall of green forest high in the hill reflects over the surface of the water; the tow of barges stuck on a sandbar with its paddle-wheel tug and crew.

They had to wait several days for a heavy rain to float them free. The crew was invited to our big corn roast.

Then there was the walk over the railroad tracks and up the dirt road hill a quarter mile to Stoops' farm for milk, butter, eggs, apple butter and bread. The loaves of bread were very large, round golden mountains of dough hot right out of the outdoor beehive oven. The Stoop sisters would cut a slice of bread from a giant-size loaf, holding it against their ample bosomed chests and sawing away with an oversized carving knife. Then smear fresh butter and apple butter all over the warm bread. The milk was extra cold because it was poured from a big round rose glass pitcher afloat in the spring house.

Actually, all this begetting and begatting in the Tuttle Clan in America began some time after John Tuttle and family, with a few others, departed from Bristol, England, May 23, 1635 aboard the *Angel Gabrial*. The ship put in at Pemaquin Point on the coast of Maine, August 14. The ship was well loaded with livestock and the people with all their earthly belongings. The stench aboard must have been extremely obnoxious. The passengers and some of the crew went ashore for the night to escape the stinking ship. During the night a powerful storm descended upon them, sinking the ship and taking with it all their earthly belongings, livestock and some of the crew. The Cogswell family was there, too.

The Tuttle family managed to work their way south to Chebasco, Massachusetts near the present site of Essex and then to Dover, New Hampshire in 1638. In 1642 John Tuttle drew lot number 7 in the first division on the west bank of Back River. That farm is still worked today by a Tuttle.

Anyway, we Tuttles have been around for a few years ever since departing TUTTLE STREET by the ancient wall in OLD LONDON TOWN.

The year of my birth 1909 was a depression year and my father, a young artist, was scratching for a living for his little wife, infant son, a one-year-old daughter and two-year-old son. They had propagated themselves out of a one-bedroom, third-floor apartment next to the new high school in Wilkinsburg, Pennsylvania. They moved into the first-floor apartment on the corner of Todd and Kelly streets right where the double streetcar tracks enter the great stone tunnel under Pennwood Avenue and the railroad tracks. The tracks at that time were at street level.

I began remembering things early in life, like crawling out the bathroom window to the vacant lot next door to play in the mud; climbing to the top of the great stone retaining wall this side of the tunnel. The little four-wheeled summertime streetcars passing in line packed with screaming kids on their way to Kennywood Amusement Park. Across Kelly Street from our apartment a flight of wooden stairs leading up to Penn Wood Avenue leaned against the four-story all-wood Westinghouse Club for men. It had a very large gym, running track, locker rooms, and the Carnegie Library.

Oh yes, I remember the first Christmas Tree, it was a blur; the little puppy under the tree was not a blur, he was named Jake, and he cried most of the night. Dad could not sleep. Soooo, Dad put Jake in bed with me, that made me very happy and everyone was able to get some sleep. From then on we were best bed friends. We shared crackers in bed with the fleas. That is when my Dad decided it was time to move and my bed would no longer be a fleabag.

We moved to 517 Kelly Street, just up the hill to Hay Street and half a block further on. Jake had grown rapidly and was man enough to take over the duties of Watch Dog. Jake was the spitting image of the dog pictured on Victor Records. He was the terror to the mailman, milkman and any uniform. He was a friend to every tramp, beggar and bum that came down the street. He even had lunch with them!

Many of my life's stories had their origin in the embrace of the loving family living in this old frame house at 517 Kelly in Wilkinsburg, Pennsylvania. Dad and Mother added my kid sister, Sweety, about eight years later and our kid brother, Spike, twelve years after that. Spike (William Bernard) was ten pounds at birth and continued to outgrow us all in size and brains.

Mother and Dad were the most wonderful people in the world. How they managed to keep their family together through adversities they encountered is a miracle of love.

We five kids attended the Wilkinsburg Kelly School, Junior High School and High School. Then Dad and Mother sent Bud to Pitt, Helen and Sweety to Carnegie, me to Washington and Jefferson College, and Spike to Penn State and Pitt. Spike and I attended Hahnemann Medical College and Hospital and joined the U.S. Armed Services. Spike served during WWII in the Navy and the Korean War in the Air Force

Well, I could go on writing some more but there is not enough time left after ninety years to record the mundane.

Just read some of the high points for the fun of it.

Father Heath and Mother Florence

9

For the Love of Lucy

My, how I can remember those happy times long ago. At the time it did not seem so happy but more like an ordeal. You really have to go back in time for this one. This is about the early 'fifties.

The explosion of homes into the expanding suburbia had skipped over our ridge of hills where we had four aching acres of weeds and trees. The new residents — all young and energetic – were wasting no time producing what was to become known as the baby boomers. The baby boomers with ponytails were well on their way to growing up and really wanting things.

A new shopping center had spawned itself a mile or so from our home. We had been driving miles into town to shop at the nearest A&P grocery store. This new shopping center with wide areas of free parking was most convenient for residents in the expanding community. Families flocked there with all their broods of baby boomers.

The bustling new businesses had a big promotional raffle underway to celebrate the grand opening in May of that year. The first, and only prize in the July drawing was a beautiful, shaggy, moth-eaten Texas burro, all black with gray around the nose and eyes. A nasty open gash from a rope burn adorned her neck. This should have been a signal or notice that she had a mind of her own. The poor animal had been manhandled roughly, probably because she was so stubborn or frightened. The flesh wound should have been a sign of trouble to come.

The burro was in the parking lot ensconced in a small corral of snow fence surrounded by kids. To help assure there would be a winner, the merchants gave free entry tickets with each purchase. These were to be signed with name, address, and phone number. We had a large number of free chances because my dear wife bought like there would be a famine tomorrow.

The rule was, only parents' signatures would be accepted. This ruling resulted in my dear wife signing hundreds of lottery tickets — name, address, and phone number — to silence the clamoring of my youngest daughter who was then 6 years old. Dear little Lucy really needed something to ride on. After all, her big sister Corine had a real horse. Lucy had to wait forever for a ride as her big sister always decided the horse was too tired or needed a bath just when Lucy wanted a ride. So it was really true. Lucy needed something to ride on. Lucy was absolutely certain about the outcome of the drawing and all during May and June announced that she would win the donkey!

Sure enough, at noon, July 1, the telephone rang. I answered the call to learn that we, of all people, were the proud winners of a Texas burro. This announcement was followed by a real plaintive voice, "WON'T YOU PLEASE TAKE HER"! I do know that there was a Hell-of-a-lot of sensible people living in our suburbia. I was not one of them. You never saw a situation quite like this on TV. This animal was for real.

Our youngest was levitated, ecstatic, thrilled and very contagious spreading the excitement through the family and nearby neighbors. So the whole family jumped into the station wagon and rushed over to the shopping center to retrieve the prize. Lucy had already named the burro Brighty after a burro named Bright Angel in a children's story of a burro in the Grand Canyon.

A rickety old horse trailer arrived to transport this poor shaggy, lovely, moth-eaten, stubborn beast to our home. After much pushing, pulling, and grunting by the crowd of city cowboys the animal was aboard headfirst. The door closed. Brighty punctuated the fact with a solid kick to the door.

The resulting racket awakened me from a dream world. I was supposed to be a dignified surgeon, oozing confidence, intelligence, and captain of the ship *Aurora*.

This should not be happening to me. What a self-taught jerk! She, the donkey, not my wife, had not responded the right way to our first loving, gentle advances. Where in the world were we going to put this animal once we got it home? As usual, my dearly beloved had the answer to the problem: "Put her in the backyard."

Several years before this, I, the would-be master of the house, had constructed a 40 foot square wire fence enclosure off the kitchen door to prevent our small children and dogs from wandering off into the tall weeds around the property. The fence was no longer of any use since our elder daughter, Corine, had taught our big dog to jump the fence. I had always wanted to remove that eyesore, but "Mother knows best." (Now I realize she has not disposed of anything we might have a need for in the future. I cannot open a closet door without causing an avalanche.) She never throws anything away so the fence remained in place. She was very proud of this fence — this hunk of junk. My dearly beloved retorted gleefully, "See, I told you we would have a need for that fence some day!"

So now you know where this bedraggled, smelly animal was ensconced — right in our backyard outside the kitchen door.

Well, it did not take long for this sweet little smelly beast to find out where all the goodies came from. She just stood right by the kitchen door and NICKERED until the

Lucy with her prize donkey, Brighty and older sister, Corine standing by.

I'm smiling here, but little did I realize what had I gotten myself into.

door opened and out would come carrots, apples, dog biscuits, and other treats.

So, my wife and I realized that we needed to build a stable for Brighty and our elder daughter's horse.

July passed with little or no rain. The barn was still in the paper stage of plans. A backyard dust bowl ensued. In one corner of the enclosure Brighty stood to sleep. In the second corner she stood to observe the activity of the neighborhood. In the third corner Brighty stood by the kitchen door when she wanted to be fed. In the fourth corner, near the rose garden, she crapped. The proximity to the rose garden was notably convenient.

The roses became the recipients of all the road apples Brighty could produce. If you do not know what a road apple is, you will after

you have stepped on one and it oozes up between your toes, atomizing an unmistakable odor into the atmosphere.

Now you know why we had the most beautiful roses in the neighborhood! (A practical application of recycling.) My daughters always said that every time their mother returned from the garden club show with a blue ribbon for her roses, their father kissed Brighty on the nose.

The story I am telling you may sound like a soap opera. Just believe me — a soap opera it is NOT. The story is true. Brighty can sing — this is for real. Brighty never sang opera even though she may have been in the Elixir of Love.

August was ushered in with a gigantic towering thunderstorm. At 2 A.M. I had just escaped into my side of a two-car garage just ahead of the blast — wind whipping me as I raised and lowered the door. Upstairs I collapsed into bed after long hours of emergency surgery. Sleep was all I needed to restore energy needed for the busy day ahead. I even prayed for sleep after everything else I had thanked the Good Lord for — but to no avail.

In bounded my dearest little Lucy screaming at the top of her voice, "Daddy! Daddy get up! Brighty is going to get all wet and struck by lightning!" That donkey had been born and raised in the western great plains. She had never seen or been in a barn. But with such pleading from a little one, what else is a father to do but get his butt out of the warm bed. OH, GREAT JEHOSHA-PHAT!

So, out of my bed into my slippers, I went down the hall, the stairs, out the garage door, into the darkness, gusts of wind and flashes of lightning to retrieve Lucy's burro from our fenced-in backyard. I dashed up the terrace, through the gate, to find Brighty standing in the shimmering, heavenly lightning way over in the farther corner near the roses. Her rear-end was toward me — I still did not know whether she would kick me, so I advanced with great trepidation, tip-toeing to prevent soiling my nice slippers in fresh road apples.

I managed to grab her little halter. Brighty refused to move. The wind was increasing. The first big drops of rain splashed off the top of my head. Air-to-ground lightning and thundering flashed and crashed about us everywhere. Pulling sideways, I forced Brighty to go in circle after circle, making our way across the enclosure until we arrived at the gate where she just stood — immovable.

At this point the rain really began coming down. Out of desperation and with great anxiety, and total stupidity, I got behind her, grabbed both hind legs, and gave a mighty shove. Through the gate we went, but no further. She stopped at the top of the terrace where I was able to grab hold of her flimsy halter with both hands. I had the downhill advantage so I gave a mighty hard pull. The darn halter broke. I landed on my back on the sodden cracked stone driveway. There I lay in agony, looking through pouring rain at that perfectly ugly beast wagging her ears at me. In spite of the burning sensation in my back, I struggled to my feet, slithered up the embankment, grabbed dear Brighty by the neck where we stood in the downpour, immobilized in the flood of light from the bedroom windows above the garage doors.

All the while, my dear wife had been hanging out of the bedroom window over the garage, screaming instructions to me through the roar of the storm. She claims instructions to me are never heeded. I did this time! She was screaming "Twitch her nose!" Hell's Fire, I did not know what TWITCH meant in horsey language. My wife is a horse expert. I put on my dumb look for explanation. In response she in true form began twisting her own nose.

Dutifully, I grabbed Brighty's nose and twisted. I hung around her neck and kept twisting, shouting sweet nothings into her ear. We proceeded to the garage door where she refused to budge. My car was there. Hail was stinging my back and bouncing off my head. While Brighty contemplated the back of my car, I TWITCHED even harder and whispered more sweet nothings into her ear. Still, no movement was forthcoming.

While Brighty was mesmerized by the rear end of my car, I got about ten yards from the back of her and charged, throwing my shoulder into her rump. She leapt into the garage

Le Docteur et l'ane - AL5972 A.D 1972

Parkway. Heavenly days, I did not awaken until 8 A.M.

At this point you must be introduced to the standard characteristics of an Operating Room Supervisor. These gals are a breed of women unto themselves. Absolute monarchs of their territory, they are the most imperious bitches this side of Hell. They are the terror of all surgeons who, early in their careers, learn that in the eyes of their Operating Room Supervisor, they are merely ***MALE CHAUVINISTIC PIGS*** of the lowest order.

Believe me, I was frightened when I awakened at 8 A.M. and it was not a nightmare. It was real! "Wake up!" I hurriedly roused my wife. "Call the Operating Room and tell them I have been delayed."

I jumped out of bed and into my clothes. Down the stairs, into the garage and through donkey dung (DD for short) and urine on the floor. The stench was overpowering.

To get out of the garage was impossible. Brighty had placed herself between the garage door and the rear end of my car. I could not get past Brighty to open my side of the garage.

First, I called to my wife for help. Then quickly I found a rope, a piece of my wife's clothesline, to put around Brighty's neck. This accomplished, I opened the other garage door behind Louise's car, stepped into the pouring rain to open the garage door from the outside to my car and Brighty.

That was good progress, but Brighty would not budge. No way was she going out into the rain.

At that moment my better half arrived to the rescue in her beautiful silken robe and little gold slippers sloshing, sliding and tiptoeing through fresh DD and U. We both began pulling and pushing at this immovable beast. Time was wasting, so out of despera-

and stood between the two cars with her rear end toward me. I got the garage door down, but was faced with the dilemma of getting past Brighty's rear end. Her head was turned my way with her ears way down. Her eyes seemed to be taking an aim on me for planting a few kicks. No way was I going up that blind alley. So, I had to go around the other side of my car and climb over the hood to get into the house. Finally, dried off and in clean dry PJs, I collapsed into bed at 4 A.M. No prayers for sleep were needed this time!

The story ain't over yet. I had an 8 A.M. operation scheduled at the hospital. Surgeons had to be there by 7:30 A.M., scrubbed, gowned, and ready by 8 A.M. That meant that I had to be out of bed and on my way before 6:30 A.M., battling the flow of traffic, which always seemed to be parked on the

tion I squeezed past into my car and backed out, pushing my beloved spouse and Brighty into the rain. I had never seen my wife's eyes get so big. Brighty and Louise looked so forlorn standing in the rain as I waved good-bye. There was only one humane thing for me to do — maneuver the car around to push them back into the garage.

Arriving at the hospital at 9 A.M. to face the wrath of an irate Operating Room Supervisor had me shuddering. After pleading my case, and never once trying to make an excuse, she finally consented to let me proceed. I could not have told her the truth — it would have taken too much time — and she would not have believed me anyway.

The procedure was going very well. The patient, under spinal anesthetic, and nurses and OR crew listened with rapt attention as I told them what had delayed me that morning. Just as we were applying the plaster and dressings, who should come bustling into my operating room but the OPERATING ROOM SUPER-VISOR. Standing at the foot of the table, she was mad and she shouted in the most imperious voice, "NOW DOCTOR, WHAT IS THE EXCUSE THIS TIME?"

So I told her the truth.

"I COULD NOT GET MY ASS OUT OF THE GARAGE!"

What happened next you would never believe. The room exploded with laughter. The anesthesiologist rolled off his stool, my patient almost rolled onto the floor, and Sue, my scrub nurse, disappeared under the operating table. Do you think my dear supervisor could ever forgive me? Well, she did. Because she was a wonderful good sport and tops among Operating Room Supervisors.

See who came to our house for breakfast, lunch and dinner

Snake Stories-
For My Grandson AJ

Suliot Farm House, 1995. Now a historical landmark. 1881 – 1991 Poplars.

About 1915, when I was six, just your age now, AJ, I was summering on a farm over there in Salem, Ohio. My Father, your Great-Grandfather, sent the family to this farm to escape the danger of polio epidemics that occurred all too often in the cities in those days. Your Great-Grandmother, Great-Uncle Heath, whom we called Bud, and your Great-Aunt Helen, were all there. Bud was nine, Helen was eight, and I was six going on seven.

The farm was owned and worked by the Suliot family—grand old Quakers. The first day of our arrival we kids were greeted by the little old grandmother clad in a long gray dress and a tiny gray bonnet. She was sitting in a great wooden rocking chair way back in the shade of a very large vine-shrouded porch. She gathered us in her arms and told us the rules for kids: 1) No fires; 2) Close all doors and gates and lock them, 3) When the big bell on the top of that high pole rings, you come at once to the house for meals.

So you see, we were free to have a wonderful time. I know I did because I have hundreds of stories to tell you.

During our first summer vacation on the farm I had several experiences with garden snakes, black snakes, and blue racers. The blue racers were six feet long. At home I had such a big mouth for bragging. I tried to impress the kids back home with exaggerated snake stories. Of course these friends did not believe me. They were already street smart, and at that tender age understood the meaning of BS. If you do not understand the meaning of that abbreviation, just ask your Dad or better yet, ask your Mother. She learned the meaning of it listening to your Dad.

It was the very last day of the second summer vacation on the farm when the story about snakes got started. Early that morning I had been down in the pastures, bringing in the cows. All I had to do was walk behind them, the cows were already heading for the barn. They knew the routine better than I, but it did make me feel important.

On the path was a gigantic round pink granite boulder. It had been left there as the ice melted at the end of the ICE AGE. On top of it was 6 feet of black snake all coiled up, glistening in the sun. (The length of the snake gets longer with each telling.) What a beautiful specimen!

We had been told to leave them alone because the snakes were our best friends. (I questioned that wisdom because women scream and run with their dresses pulled up above their knees.)

Well, I captured that snake. I thought that I had killed it, so I grabbed him by the

Suliot Barn, 1995, me with grandchildren, Penny & AJ

tail and began pulling it along the ground. I discovered at once that it would not pull that way. The scales stuck to everything. Pulling the snake by the neck was easier. I headed for the spring house

Reaching the old spring house, I put the dead serpent into a bucket to keep it cool in the water so I could show it to my brother Bud and sister Helen. After breakfast, Bud and Helen came to the spring house and had a good look at the snake. It looked quite comfortable in the bucket.

At that point in time, mother called me to bathe and dress for the trip home. This was done in mother's room on the second floor of the big house. I had to stand in that big washbowl with the painted flowers on it as mother scrubbed me down. That is when I saw the open suitcase on her bed. My dear mother was finishing all the packing. One suitcase was always left open on the bed to put all loose little last-minute things.

The idea struck me of showing the big snake to my friends back home. I now had the perfect vehicle to transport the truth of my big snake stories back home for close inspection.

Dressed and ready for the trip to the train station, I had time to retrieve my dead snake from the spring house. Gathering it up in my arms and hands, I wrapped the snake around my body so I would not get it dirty dragging it along the ground. Everyone in the house was so busy they did not notice what I was doing.

The suitcase was still open. I coiled the snake up real nice on top of all those white clothes. It looked real (live) honestly. The case was full, so I put the lid down. That chore done, I went down the stairs and out onto the big front porch to swing in that big lawn swing.

Soon after that I heard a blood-curdling scream and then another rendition followed by yet another vocalist then a chorus of screams. A calamity had just begun.

A gaggle of stampeding, shrieking, terrified women came stumbling down the steps, crushing through the screen door, scurrying across the wide verandah onto the lawn where they went prancing wildly around in circles with their long dresses over their heads. Just like an Indian War dance!

After watching this calamity in progress I went upstairs to see what all the commotion was about. The snake was no longer on top of the clean white clothes in the suitcase.

Those crazy women must have scared the hell out of that poor snake!

Well, you wanted to know how I remembered this story—I CAN FEEL IT. You know darn well what happened to me. I can still feel it. I will never forget that snake story as long as I live. Why? Here's the truth:

"If your mother ever spanked you as hard as my mother swatted my little behind you would never forget why you got spanked."

Was the snake really dead? No way! He was just pretending.

The History of Wild Oats

Oats have been spread indiscriminately and consistently for centuries by the young and the old. To observe the gonadaltrophic action upon the adolescent male is a revelation. To the young male the amorous attraction to the opposite sex is an exciting, wonderful experience for him. His responses to these primordial forces are natural. But who can explain the actions of the young man with fuzz on his lip acting like a whooping crane doing his mating dance.

Sooo, what's new? It's always new to the young crop and don't you forget it! You cannot always participate but you can always observe and remember the goings-on of romance of puppy love.

Some crops of later (older) teens were vintage and unforgettable. Oh, how I remember observing. Now I will not "kiss and tell" as the whole town saw this story unfold one evening in the high school auditorium way back there in the mid-twenties.

One of our senior fellows was quite the Don Juan. Tall, lanky and beaked nose, he sang tenor too. He always sang tenor in every high school operetta production. Invariably, the operetta would be a Gilbert & Sullivan classic — *The Mikado* or *The Pirates of Penzance*.

This year it happened to be *The Pirates of Penzance* and our Don Juan was to be the lead because he was the only one who could sing tenor. He was greatly pleased when the leading lady was to be the sweetest, most lovely bit of feminine pulchritude that forever brings back the desire to be young again.

Our Don Juan lost no time trying to make time with this beauty. All his advances to her were blunted, met with queenly censorial rebuke.

The costuming for this show had the boys in leotards for some unknown reason. The costumes did not arrive for the dress rehearsal. However, the leotards arrived for opening night. Athletic supporters had not been supplied. The result was quite revealing. I should say "a spectacular testicular revelation".

From the girls' point of view the chance to get all rouged up, lips painted red, was quite a thrill — almost sinful. The dean of women in the high school forbade rouge, lipstick and chewing gum. This was a chance to flaunt themselves in defiance of the law. They really were breathtakingly beautiful. The leading lady was the most beautiful of them all.

Our tenor's spindly shanked legs were not the most sexually tantalizing spectacle that ever crossed a stage. Wearing leotards was a new experience for these easily aroused studs.

Our greatest tenor was to sing his love song to the sweetest, beautiful leading lady. Being truly ladylike, she had shrugged off Don's ardent play for her attention throughout all the rehearsals. Don was actually quivering with anticipation by the first night of the performance, particularly when he saw how gorgeously beautiful was the leading lady all painted and rouged.

That first night our own group of adolescent delinquents was sitting in the front row of the balcony, our chins on the brass rail. We were quite proud of our friends performing so well. Don's voice was really projecting.

He could really sing. The voices blended beautifully. Things went very well until the love scene where Don and the first lady were to stand in the center stage about as close together as the dean of women would allow.

The first lady was dazzling, all painted up. Thrilling with excitement, she weakened to Don's ardent protestation. At first contact she responded with queenly dignified acquiescence and then erupted into energetic cooperation in the middle of the performance, but not on the stage. This ardent eruption occurred just outside the stage door on the steps, where energetic cooperation, hugging and kissing occurred.

Time flies all too fast during such hormonal reactions. The orchestra began repeating the same music over and over again. Something was wrong. Don and the female lead did not appear as in the rehearsal.

The excited stage manager dashed out to untangle the couple from this ardent entanglement shouting, "You're supposed to be on stage!"

So upon the stage they bounced. The first lady, all smiles of delight with the thrills of conquest, dragging poor Don behind with his face smeared with lipstick. His voice projected exceedingly well as did his joy stick making an amazingly large tent in front of his leotards which he tried to conceal by half turning his back to the audience while twisting his neck out of joint, showing his lipstick-smeared face to the assembled townspeople. Turned in that way (in profile) the tent became more evident to both audience and the grinning, snickering chorus. The tittering of the girls in the chorus was heard over the lover's duet. Don's voice cracked only once when the first lady made a sharp gesture downward inadvertently striking and deflating the tent pole.

So, as I said in the beginning, I am not kissing and telling. The whole town saw it! We can always observe the goings-on of romance and the attempts of some to sling about a wild oat or two. Remembering is a joy too. It is fun for the young to hear and the old to tell over and over again this happy bit of history!

Skippy Loved Change

In our town where I grew up we were fortunate to have a grand old dry goods store. This venerable store had been in business a very long time, more that fifty years before I was born. The customers could sit down on little stools at the counter and be waited on by dear little old gray-haired clerks who knew the merchandise and most of the gossip about town, all things measurable and unmentionable.

In this great emporium of needles, buttons, and pins, nested along with old ladies' winter long johns and summer underwear, you could find all those things which could not be found anywhere else in the world. So all the ladies of the town would inform you that store was really up-to-date, just like in Kansas City.

The little metal cash boxes clicked, clanged and banged, propelled in constant motion along a rod cage or shaft rattling back and forth from several counter stations to the cashier sitting in the balcony.

Mother asked me to go up the street to buy sewing needs in the old dry goods store. Skip, the fraternity dog who had been turned over to me and my family for summer vacation, and I headed off. We were inseparable. Skip and I entered the store, right past the big sign "NO DOGS ALLOWED." Skippy could not read even though she had attended college for two years. I know some guys who still cannot read after four years of college. They played football.

Once inside the store, Skippy spied the change boxes whizzing about and gave chase, barking and yelping in boundless excitement.

She flew up the wide stairs to the cashier's balcony and back down the stairs. A cacophony of screaming erupted from the women. The proprietor, Mr. Caldwell, joined the commotion, chasing Skippy out the front door. She just reentered, ushering in the next customer with the swing of the door, to start the racket and confusion all over again.

Trying with all my might to disown her, she kept returning to me, looking for a moment of approval. Though I tried to ignore and disown Skip, Mr. Caldwell saw through my subterfuge and escorted us both out the front door unceremoniously.

Skip loved to chase those little change boxes. Thereafter, she would get all excited when we went up the street, just anticipating a chance to chase, and per chance, catch a little change.

Summertime On
Suliot's Farm Revisited

Suliot Farm Out Buildings — Chicken Alley, watercolor by Dr. Tuttle

On that lower farm of the Suliot's, the old stone spring house was in daily use. Crocks of fresh butter, sweet milk, butter milk and sour dough sat in the flow of cold spring water in stone troughs and gurgling around the path of stepping stones zigzagging on the floor. In the cold water on the floor, one large five-gallon crock sat cooling the hard cider there. That hard stuff was from last year's fall apple crop, now well fermented.

Three or four dippers hung from the wall beside the big crock. This was the Mecca spot for the men on any hot summer day, just to sip a drop or two of the tasty brew or fill a

small jug using the little funnel so handily hung by the dippers.

One hot Saturday afternoon, Dad and his friend Garber, from Boggs and Bule's Department Store, were thirsting for a wee bit of cool refreshment and wandered down to the old spring house, which was about a mile from the big house. They each filled a large glass stein with this delicious juice. Thus fortified, they proceeded outside to stretch themselves out on the cool grass under the big trees on the lawn in front of the spring house.

From their comfortable spot on the lawn,

they had a beautiful view across the lane and over the pasture shimmering in the heat of the day. In the right far quarter of the pasture, cattails, 6 feet tall were growing in a swamp. The cattails were taller than that, depending on how far down your legs sank into the muck. Just beyond the swamp was a large stand of 12-foot-high elderberry bushes where a footpath vanished into the woods. Mother and Grandmother Smith were mixed up in that jungle of water-loving bushes, having a wonderful time picking away at the berries for jelly they planned to make. Those two lovely ladies had a deadly fear of snakes and why they were in that snake pit of a place picking berries? Well, they didn't know what a predicament they were in!

Three hundred yards or more across the pasture from the spot these gals were in, Dad and Garber were feeling no pain, completely relaxed, flat on their backs. They did not realize how thirsty they had been or how much hard cider they had consumed to put them in such a state of exuberance. Dad's eyes finally brought into focus the movement in the bushes way over there beyond the swamp in the pasture. Dad hollered to Mother (my dad — how he could holler FLOSSIEEE). It scared me — made me jump! I was right beside him on the grass.

Mother responded by waving her straw hat and YOO-HOOING to Father who was rolling on the grass, laughing. Those poor dear women made a beeline toward us on the grass in front of the spring house. They waded right into the swampy muck and 6-foot cattails. I called to them to take the long way around, but they just kept plowing ahead and became too busy trying to get their feet out of the muck, sinking ever deeper up to their shins, as panic was setting in with a scream now and then for help from us three

men. That's when Dad HOLLERED at the top of his lungs, "SNAKES!"

That shout from Dad did it — those two lovely ladies were put into total panic. Cattails went spinning from there, churning about in the muck. The crescendo of their screams became shrieks and the shrieking turned to bellows of rage and threats of mayhem. You never saw such threshing about in that swamp.

Those two frightened gals came stomping through the muck, trampling cattails like water buffaloes, bulldozing their way right up to Dad, rolling on the lawn with laughter. There they stopped and began bashing Dad over the head with their baskets of elderberries.

Dad never stopped laughing. Garber had better sense. He extricated himself from the scene, staggering out of sight.

LET'S HAVE ANOTHER SWIG OF HARD CIDER.

Tin Lizzy

You kids have never lived until you have put together your own automobile. We did. I was about 15 years old at the time, the Roaring Twenties had just begun, and I had never been behind the wheel of a real live automobile. Our families did not have any private means of transportation. We all used public transportation — streetcars and trains.

My brother Bud and his friend Van got the idea of building their own car when they found the rear end and front end of a Model T Ford chassis complete with engine abandoned in the backyard of an old store near Coal Street and Penn Avenue. It seemed the ditch diggers (who were laying pipe) had found it more convenient to saw the chassis in half and standing it up on its ends. The boys wheeled the engine half across town about twelve blocks to our back alley. The rear half with the drive shaft arrived the same way.

When Dad found out about what they had done he had to rent a space in a corrugated metal garage next door. Parking such junk on the street was against the law. Our own back yard was the playground for the entire neighborhood — and the only one without grass or a garage.

Finally, another old chassis was found and deposited in the garage. Then came the gas tank and a 1914 radiator with the brass cover. The hood was heavy-gauge aluminum.

Bud, Van and I put the parts together and it really ran! Those two idiots tied cushions on the gas tank and drove all the way from Pittsburgh to our Lake Erie cottage, 120 miles, stopping every few miles to put water into the leaking radiator. The roads were very narrow black top, high crowded Pinchot roads, which had been laid over cow paths. Many were still mud roads, others were gravel roads. Gas stations were few and far between. After about 8 hours of driving without a windshield, faces to the wind, straining the air of flying insects with their teeth, they got that rolling junk pile 2 miles from the cottage along the lake road where it collapsed and sat beside the old gravel road for several days. Bud and Van had been too busy chasing girls to worry over their mechanical miracle.

Sam Cooper, a graduate student at the University of Pittsburgh, doing work in chemistry, was my neighbor at the lake. He had the use of a big new Studebaker sedan that belonged to his family. A mechanical engineer he was not.

Sam and I decided it would be best to tow that wreck off the side of the road to our backyard at the cottage. We absconded with my Mother's clothesline for our tow rope, climbed into the new Studebaker and set off down the road to retrieve the pile of junk before someone else claimed our wreck for salvage.

There it was! Being forever intrepid and stupid, we secured the tow line to the Fliver. I planted my bottom on the pillow secured to the gas tank. What a jerk! I had never driven a motorized vehicle in my life. I did not know what the three pedals on the floor were for, nor did I know that the left hand brake lever had three functions. I did not know how to start or stop. I had never driven a Model T before.

What I did learn later was that the brake handle, when pulled all the way back, was the parking and emergency brake. Halfway forward was neutral. All the way forward was high gear.

Those three foot pedals on the floor of the Model T Ford are unique. The left pedal when pressed all the way forward puts the car into low gear as long as you keep pressing hard. Halfway forward is neutral and all pressure off you have the car in high gear. The middle pedal puts the car in reverse when pressed hard to the floor as long as the car is in neutral. Remember, brake handle halfway forward or left pedal halfway forward. The right pedal is the brake — just press it hard as you put the car in neutral.

This junker did not have a key to the ignition. A Model T had to be cranked to start the motor or it could be started by towing. The accelerator is a little hand lever under the steering wheel on the left. All the way up is slow. All the way down is full speed ahead. The right handle, the spark, was the same: all the way up, ready for hand cranking start and all the way down, full speed ahead.

Now that you have reviewed the instructions for driving a Model T Ford I do not recommend that you jump into a Tin Lizzy for a trial run unless you are in a ten-acre empty parking lot. Do it stupidly as I did and you may not live to tell of your fright.

Without such knowledge and practice to our credit, we started down that old dusty gravel road, spark handle and gas handle in their down position (full speed ahead). It is a wonder that the gods paid any attention to us at all.

Sam yelled, "Let off the brake!" Dutifully, I responded to the command — and that put me in high gear. Towing in gear started the engine — and after a few explosions that pile

of junk and I were in full chase, tied to Sam's (father's) new Studebaker, and he was trying desperately to get away from me. In a cloud of dust, flying stones and steam, we sped down the road — me hanging on for dear life.

Speed? **** B.S.! We were going like HELL BENT FOR ELECTION! Sam kept speeding up to keep away from me. The faster he went so did the scrap heap. In his haste to get away from me he forgot I was tied to him — a prisoner of his speed.

Sam made a fast turn into our lane thinking I would go straight ahead. But the tow line jerked that pile of scrap behind him where it bounced to a stop a few inches from Sam's new car rear bumper, thanks to me, pressing all three foot pedals to the floor, but there was no floor!

I was stiff with fright. My arms were braced on the wheel and my legs fully extended. I could see Sam jump out of his car to inspect the damage. None found, he came over to inspect the carnage. Sam pried my hands from the steering wheel. He lifted me bodily off the gas tank and tried to stand me on two feet. My knees collapsed, not necessarily in supplication to the Almighty. Sam kept sniffing around me, thinking I might have had an inside accident.

The adventures had just begun.

Well, anyway, I am here to tell you about Lizzy's leaking radiator; about the leaking radiator, many remedies have been tried. None of these myths will produce the desired result. All you have to do is buy a new radiator or a second-hand one. Money we did not have. The bottom of the Depression was still with us.

I had heard the alternative to buying a new radiator was to put some oatmeal into the radiator. It all seemed reasonable. The boiling water would make a mush of the oatmeal, thus plugging the holes in the radiator. This stuffing of oatmeal into the radiator was done with great gusto and confidence. For the moment the leaking ceased. So we had to try the results with a test run.

We set off down the road. That Fliver fairly frothed at the mouth, splattering our faces with globs of boiling oatmeal. Obviously, that remedy was a total failure. We managed to return, pushing that rattletrap to our launching pad to try another remedy.

Then some (SOB) A-HOLE suggested we put a can of powdered mustard into the radiator. We were stupid enough to do it. Obviously, our ardent love affair with this Tin Lizzy was waning rapidly. Well, we cranked her up and away we went for another test run. She began to heat up rapidly, blowing steam and chunks of oatmeal mixed with mustard gas. Forced to a rapid halt, our exposed parts were aflame and our eyes blinded by the mustard. We rushed to the nearest roadside puddle to dunk the burning sensation.

The only thing we could say about this futile effort to plug a leaking radiator was that we reinvented mustard gas. It is a wonder we survived.

But, I am here, a testament to the promise of the Lord to take care of us whether we deserved it or not. I am here, ain't I?

Jake The Dog And
Billy The Goat At 517 Kelly

The first dog we had in the family was a Fox Terrier. Just a little thing, as I remember. We were living on the first floor of a three-story apartment building facing Todd Street at the corner with Kelly Street in Wilkinsburg. That is where Kelly Street goes through the large stone tunnel under Penn Wood Avenue and the Pennsylvania Railroad. Off the kitchen door there was the great stone retaining wall to climb. Across Kelly from the apartment was a long high wooden stairway up to Penn Wood. There also was the Westinghouse Club for men. It had a large gym, a banked running track, handball courts, and a Carnegie Library. This was a large wooden structure.

My older brother and sister, Bud and Helen, and Mother and Dad, moved up Kelly Street, one block and a half to 517 in about 1912 when Wilson was President. I liked Teddy Roosevelt, because he was a cowboy.

Five Hundred Seventeen Kelly was a big, all wood three-story house with a front and back yard. Neighboring homes on each side were just like it, but painted differently. Each house had a living room, dining room, kitchen, pantry, hallway, six bedrooms, and one bath, with minor differences. The cellars were paved. The heating systems were all different. Ours was hot air, coal fired. Each residence had, on the inside, a back stairway to the second floor leading from the kitchen to the second floor. Each had front stairs to the second floor and stairs to the third floor. I certainly knew the layout, I had been in them all.

Jake made the move with the family and immediately took over the security duties. He was a steadfast friend of mine and the perfect enemy of our postman and delivery-man. Old tramps and beggars were excluded from Jake's list of bitables. In his early puppy days, when first introduced to our family, he cried so much at night mother and dad could not sleep. In desperation, they put Jake in bed with me, much to my delight; every night in my bed—fleas and all. It's no wonder we were referred to as bed fast friends. WHEN JAKE HAD WORMS—SO DID I.

One day we had to restrain Jake from attacking the deliverymen who were trying to carry a Victor phonograph into the living room. This thing was advertised as a Victrola with the sound so perfect it was "Just like the masters voice." A dozen flat round records with Jake's Picture in the middle of each one arrived to add to the confusion. The neighborhood kids and we three kids loved to play "The Whistler and His Dog" over and over just to hear Jake bark in response to the whistle and the barking of the dog at the end of the recording. Jake became conditioned to bark at the first whistle. So did Mother. As soon as Mother would hear the whistle she would bark at us, "Get out of the house!" It is a wonder how she put up with us. No wonder we loved her so much.

Billy the goat was another surprise. Billy arrived in our backyard at 517 towed in with a rope around his neck by Paa Dobson. Mother and Dad had just left for a 2-week second honeymoon aboard a Great Lakes steamer. (Note how carefully I marked the second honeymoon, after all, Dad was my mother's first husband.) Our babysitter was Ann Dobson, mother's friend from the second floor of the apartment building on Todd Street where she lived with her dad, Paa.

Mr. Dobson was a huge-bellied, jolly engineer who drove the Red Arrow — 10 P.M.—express to Altoona, on its way to New York. He always tooted his whistle as he thundered through Wilkinsburg at 50 mph. I remember him well because he would pinch and tease me to make me say "bullshit". Then Ann would wash my mouth out with soap. Then Paa would roar with delight. The soap washing remedy never cured me completely.

Anyway, it was Paa Dobson who deposited the goat as a gift to our backyard. We named him Billy. Billy was about 3 feet tall at the shoulders, all white with short, curved, blunt horns. The horns were good handles to wrestle with anytime he wanted to practice butting. He was the center of attraction at once, and enjoyed it just as much as all the other kids in the neighborhood, in our backyard.

The shanty we kids had built in our backyard was Billy's home. We kids had constructed this shack of scrap from the house being torn down at South Avenue and the new Wilkinsburg Station, to make way for the new extension for Penn Wood Avenue. That street was paved with wood paving blocks. That in itself is another story, because when it got damp, automobiles became uncontrollable, a real lawyer's trap.

Billy had been with us for a week when a real English Bull dog visited our backyard and attached himself to Billy's neck on the underside and hung on with clamped jaws. We could not make him let go. Poor Billy just stood there "BAH-BAAING" pitifully. Ann and the neighboring ladies screeched. The

owner of the dog rushed up with a bucket of water and dumped it on the dog's face with no effect. I turned on the garden hose and directed the flow right up the dog's nose, he just had to let go of Billy's neck. Ann washed Billy's neck and put a bandage around his neck. Billy survived this attack, and revived rapidly none the worse. During all this commotion, Jake had sense enough to stay out of it. They continued to play and sleep together.

Mother, upon returning from vacation, was not what you might refer to as happy to find an unwanted goat at her house. Dad thought it was great fun and ordered a sulky from Sears & Roebuck's catalog. A few days later a large package arrived from which the parts of a sulky were spread out on the back alley bricks. A scramble of my big brother's friends were attempting to put it all together. The sulky finally took shape with no parts left over. The harness was another puzzlement. If the goat had only stood still it would not have been such a perplexing problem.

The goat was finally harnessed to the sulky with my brother Bud seated upon the sulky, but Billy would not move. I had been pushed out of this put-together business when Mother called me from the kitchen. I responded reluctantly because I wanted to be there when Billy made his first move. Mother gave me a short list of things to get for her at Charter's Grocery Store at the corner of Hay and Rebecca, just around the corner. I took off at a run passing brother Bud on the sulky. My dog Jake at the other end of the alley saw me and gave chase.

As Jake passed Billy, he took a nip of him—Billy took after Jake full speed. Bud was hanging on for dear life; the parade rounded the corner of the alley and Hay at phenomenal speed, then bounced over the curb at Rebecca, right into Charter's, over the sawdust floor in front of the butcher's counter into the grocery department beyond. The goat wound up with his head in the cabbage basket. Jake stole a large bone from under the butcher block and went out the door in front of the butcher in hot pursuit with cleaver in hand. This scandalous happening was the talk of the neighborhood.

Billy loved to beg food at the kitchen screen door where his insistent "bah-baaing" exasperated my mother when she was too busy to hand out a tidbit. One day Mother just banged the kitchen door in his face. Well that was just more than Billy could tolerate. He went back to the middle of the yard, turned toward the kitchen door and charged, head down. He crashed through the screen door and one panel of the door, landing in the middle of the kitchen floor. Mother booted him out in no uncertain terms. HE NEVER DID THAT AGAIN!

The neighbors next door had had enough and moved away. I did not really know why

Jake the Dog, Billy the Goat, Cat, and me.

because they were the ones who had the smelly chicken coop at the end of their backyard.

That house was just like ours. It had an entrance hallway with a straight stairway to the second floor. At its side, the hallway continued back to a door to the pantry. The first door to the left opened to the living room, the second door to the left opened to the dining room. A bay window bulged from the side of the house from the dining room. A fireplace with a mantle piece 5 feet from the floor separated the dining room from the kitchen.

The stage has been set for the coming attraction of the first house hunter. She just happened to be a well-groomed lady asking Mother for the key to the house next door. Mother did not accompany the lady because she was too busy. Anyway, the house was empty. There was nothing to walk off with.

The next thing we heard from the lady was a murderous shriek. Mother and I dashed over to the house next door to administer first aid. We found this poor frightened soul standing on the 8-inch wide mantel, 5 feet off the floor, still shrieking; "WHAT WAS THAT? WHAT WAS THAT?" Mother asked, "WHAT WAS WHAT?" The spooked woman screamed back, "WHAT WAS THAT WHITE THING THAT WENT UP THE STEPS?" Mother had to tell her, "THAT WAS OUR GOAT."

Needless to say, our prospective neighbor was not interested in moving next to such neighbors as we folks.

Every day or two I had to pick up tin cans from our backyard. The common knowledge in those days was that GOATS ATE TIN CANS. The Mickey kids used our back alley on their way to school. As they passed our backyard, they always tossed in a can or two to see if the rumor was true. Since the cans were always picked up they continued to believe the rumor to be true.

We always blamed the Mickey kids for everything. In the backyard shanty we kids had constructed bunks and all-wood flooring. The furnishings were a small chair and table. The pride of all the girls was Mother's small cast-iron wood-burning cook stove. Four holes on top with covers and a real oven. The girls loved to cook and frequently served hot meals. The smoke from the stove was vented out the alley side of the shack. When the girls were busy on the inside making smoke to the outside, the Mickey kids on the outside would put a flat board over the chimney. The smoke filled the shack and the shack would empty just like a disturbed hornet's nest and just as mad.

In the early days at 517, the doors were never locked and usually left open all day in the summertime. Our neighbors were community minded. When Mother had to go downtown shopping in Pittsburgh, she would just ask the next-door neighbor to keep an eye on her brood while she was away for a few hours, upstreet or uptown going to the local business area. Downtown was Pittsburgh. We kids were well behaved enough to be trusted to stay close to home. After all, that was where all the fun and playmates were.

Well, one of the kids in our neighborhood happened to be our goat who assumed he was people and would wander into the house if the screen door was left open. One day my mother came home after shopping and found our Billy the goat asleep on top of the upright piano in the living room. Mother took a broom to Billy in no uncertain terms. Billy never did that again. WHO SAYS CORPORAL PUNISHMENT DOESN'T WORK?

Another day the boys were erecting a small

wall tent in the backyard at 517. All the kids in the neighborhood were involved, stretching the ropes and canvas, pounding in stakes and holding poles upright. Fatty Nedam from down the street was busily pounding a stake in front of the tent when he noticed Billy chewing away at a tent flap. Fatty interrupted Billy with a swift kick to the rump. That darn goat took offense to this interruption. Sooo, when Fatty bent over to continue pounding the stake, Billy took advantage of this opportunity to charge, butting Fatty's rump, pushing Fatty clear through the tent. Fatty was sore at both ends and at Billy too.

Big brother Bud had become infatuated with a sweet 8-year-old down on Hay Street somewhere. Showing early signs of normal development, he decided to experiment with what is known as flirtation. That is doing something, giving something, showing something, just to attract the attention of the first infatuation. Since Billy had been such an attraction in our backyard, Bud decided to take Billy down Hay Street to visit this first love. Bud attached a long lead rope to Billy's collar and proceeded down Hay Street. He must have been in seventh heaven when he arrived at this very young lady's house. He stood before her house, leaning against a telephone pole, shyly awaiting the reaction from within. The love bug had bitten him for the first time as the goat went around and around him. Billy had Bud securely bound to the pole. To untangle himself from this predicament, Bud had to free Billy from the collar. The show was over—Billy took off for home before Bud could get untangled. He learned that "Some days a fella just can't win."

Some days Mother just could not win. Father had ordered a nanny goat for Billy. Of course we named her Nanny. Dad had had a brainstorm concerning how to teach us kids all about the birds and the bees. I don't know why as we kids were already knowledgeable having watched numerous litters of kittens being born right under our noses. And Jake was no slouch as a stud either. Well Nanny and Billy did not hit it off at first, so nothing happened. Well almost nothing. Billy being well stimulated by Nanny began to develop (and distribute) that unique and most penetrating caprine stench of the full-grown male goat.

The neighbors had never complained too much because their kids were always in our backyard playground, the only one of its kind in town. But enough is enough, even for Mother. All good things seem to come to an end. So one day Billy was hitched to his sulky and led off by a well-dressed Italian man, with Nanny in tow behind them.

Summers at the Press Cottages Remembered

The Press cottage on the banks overlooking Lake Erie was shaped like a renaissance Chicago bungalow held off the ground with three-foot-high cement block supports. It had on the first floor a living room with brick fireplace, dining room, kitchen, and a very narrow bathroom with shower. On the second floor, it had four bedrooms separated by partitions of thin tongue and groove board walls, 8 feet high and four doors. There was no ceiling, just open air to the roof. The side walls of the cottage bungalow were flat boards nailed to 2 x 4 planks. The wind whistled through the cracks around the windows.

Accommodation of weekend crowds in the cottage required a real expert packing job—two double-decker canvas cots, three bodies to each of the three double beds, one on the couch and some on the floor.

Mother did the cooking for large crowds like that on a three-burner kerosene stove. The oven was a portable, light metal contraption that could sit on top of the stove when needed. Just how Mother managed to produce those fabulous meals was a miracle in the making each weekend.

Each Friday morning, the cottage was mopped down from top to bottom. When that was done, Mother, the girls and I would go to town shopping at the A&P, where the clerks waited upon the customers and then helped lug the loads of food stuff to the car.

That there car was the old Tin Lizzy, Model "T" Ford, the only means of transportation we had to shuttle our guests' bags and baggage from the train station to the cottage. Many of the arrivals came on the 8

P.M. train from Pittsburgh. Sometimes the trains were late, and I found myself driving after dark. The trouble was that the headlights of that Model "T" worked off the magneto and would burn out if the engine raced too fast. That happened all too often because to get moving forward, one had to press hard on the left pedal, and give the motor the gas ever so delicately. Driving Dad in the darkness was a blistering experience because of his explosiveness. It was not unusual for Dad to invite a business associate or friend to spend a weekend with his family. He had chewed me out, a real good reaming, about making sure the lights never blew out again, EVER. This extra special reaming was because of an extra special guest who was not to be subjected to any of my SHENANI-GANS, which seemed to embarrass him so much. (He always tried to look embarrassed as if it had never happened before. But I knew that look and could feel my neck wringing.)

It was in late August when the sun goes down early about 7:30 P.M. Father had called Mother about noon, and said that he would arrive at Ashtabula with this extra special guest about 8 P.M., and to remind Brother, that's me, about the headlights. I was quite apprehensive about this special guest. The poor bastard, if not forewarned of what he was getting into, was about to find himself in profound shock.

Dad had told Mother that the guest was a handsome young bachelor exploding in the business world successfully. This fact had leaked to the eligible girls and some jail bait.

As a result of this information, we set off from the cottage for this momentous rendezvous with the train at Ashtabula. With the three girls in the back seat, and Mother and I in the front seat—where in the heck was I to put Father and his special guest? They had to toss up to find out who would get out. Then the two of them tossed up to see who would sit on the guest's lap. They finally decided to fold back the canvas top onto the top of the back seat and sit on it, resting their feet on the back seat.

So off we went. At the train station, Father stepped onto the platform and conjured from behind him a tall handsome (*Homosapian erectus*) young man clothed in an immaculate sartorial conception. His dazzling smile flashed at the ladies—they damn near SWOOOONED. He had every reason to smile at those beautiful tanned long legs and smiling faces. As I saw it, his gaze became almost a lecherous leer when they turned around from him to have a better view of their rear — so voluptuous. It was a shame they had to sit on them. He was carrying a handsome leather suitcase, which the girls grabbed from him and ushered him to our transportation. When he saw our Tin Lizzy, I thought he was about to crap himself (he had probably been thinking in terms of a 12-cylinder Lincoln Town Car).

The girls tossed that beautiful leather suitcase into the V-space between the hood and the right fender. Dad tossed his old bag onto the front left fender. The girls climbed in first and sat on the folded-down top over the back seat. Dad and his hostage sat in the back seat—Mother and I up front. I was behind the wheel.

Darkness was setting in as we departed Ashtabula station. Headlights were showing up in the local traffic. Cautiously, I turned on Lizzy's lights. We were in high gear rattling along at about 20 mph just fine. Going east out of town, we turned left onto a little-used gravel road going north toward the lake. We had to cross the Nickel Plate railroad, which was a single track with no bump or hump. STOP-LOOK-AND LISTEN. With great skill I managed to get across the tracks without burning out the bulbs in the front headlights. A short distance ahead was the main line of the NEW YORK CENTRAL, four tracks wide with monstrous bumps to maneuver over. STOP-LOOK-AND LISTEN. I eased the pressure down on the left foot pedal, eased down on the throttle, and began moving the menagerie over the bumps. One bump too many caused my fingers to jerk down on the throttle. The engine roared, the light blew out as we leaped forward, bouncing high over the fourth track. The guest's suitcase tumbled off the fender and disappeared into the ditch on the right side of the road, where it burst open, scattering the contents among the weeds. The girls scrambled out of the car and in no time had literally stuffed those nice clean clothes into that suitcase and banged it back onto the right fender.

The guest's eyes must have popped out at that performance — but that was just the beginning. The last of my light bulbs had burned out so we were driving in complete darkness. I was feeling my way along that narrow high-crowned gravel road as we rolled merrily along. When the car leaned too much to the right, we were on the right side of the road, too far to the left, we were on the left side of the road. Level ride — we were in the middle of the road. The occasional on-coming car with lights on high beam could see us in plenty of time because the girls opened their *DOREINES* and faced their mirrors forward. It worked very well because one passing driver shouted "WHY DON'T YOU DIM YOUR LIGHTS!"

We finally came to the dip in the old graveled lake road where the giant willow trees make a pitch-black tunnel. That is just before we make a left turn into our lane to the cottage. ***SKUNK STENCH FILLED THE AIR!*** I must have hit it or scared the piss out of it. The whole world stunk of skunk because the permeated air became more concentrated as we reached the cottage. The damn dogs had chased that damn skunk under the cottage. To make it worse, those sprayed dogs were so happy to see us—they jumped all over us and the guest.

The guest was bewildered with nowhere to escape. He was ushered into the cottage through the large screened-in front porch to be introduced to a host of guests, friends, and neighbors. During the first onslaught of hand shaking and hugs to make him feel wanted and accepted, he escaped to the kitchen where Mother was about to open a large bottle of her homemade root beer. Mother's root beer was the explosive kind, even when well chilled. He asked to help by taking a bottle to open before Mother could demonstrate her technique. Mother always aimed the bottle into a large pitcher to let it pop and gush. The guest quickly snapped the cap off with his teeth. The explosion got him full in the face and on the ceiling. So, he had an early introduction to Mother's tricks.

The first morning our guest appeared dressed nautically in a blue blazer with brass buttons, white shirt, pants, shoes, socks, and with a white silk neckerchief—all ready for Newport yachting. Father spotted him in time and gave him a pair of his old white duck pants. Then the fun began for the day, joining the mad dash of the young crowd to the beach for tennis and monkey swinging from one limb to another in the big Oak tree. He thought he was Tarzan. He was never so happy, melting into Dad's pot. (Pot in those days was something to cook in, plant in, or poop in.)

The back porch of the cottage was screened and used as a dining area. We had made a long table and benches; each bench could seat eight people when tightly squeezed. Mother covered the table with green oilcloth large enough to hang several inches over the sides. All newcomers were given the seat of honor in the middle of the bench. We kids became quite deft at making a trough of the oilcloth in our laps directed to the middle. At a signal, water was poured in the trough from both ends. Our dear guest got the full treatment and could not escape becoming officially a truly vested member of the LONG TABLE.

Sunday evening as we loaded up the Tin Lizzy for the drive to the train station at Ashtabula, Dad's guest pleaded for the honor of driving our rattletrap. The honor was bestowed upon him, and with a flourish, his bowler at a rakish angle, he let the brake off and jerked away in a cloud of dust.

The guest confessed to Dad weeks later, that as he lay on his bed that first night in the cottage with the stench of skunk still scenting the air, he thought, "Jesus Christ Almighty! What in the Hell have I got myself into? I've joined the cast of *TOBACCO ROAD*!" But before the weekend was over, he admitted that he was playing the leading role and having the best time of his life.

The Perpetrators of many family pranks assembled at Conneaut Ohio.
From left to right: Me holding Skippy, brother Bud, Sister Helen, mother Florence
with brother Spike in front, and father Health giving sister Sweety a big hug.

Skippy The Dog's
X-Rated Remembrances

This is not a bedtime tale to be told to those under 21 years of age — it is intoxicating. In those years, anything intoxicating was illegal.

The depression years were still in full swing. Dad found it to be cheaper and more healthful for the family to summer in the Press cottage on the shores of Lake Erie. Jobs were not to be had for me — so Dad put me to work holding down the fort by the lake, keeping the 1914 Ford touring car functioning. I was picking up a buck or two transporting the girls to town from Moscoma Summer Camp for Girls, for shopping trips, and visits to the local sweet shop. The camp was operated out of the two cottages and a tent next to ours. At 25 cents for the six-mile round trip morning and afternoon, twice a week, it kept me in pocket money. I could squeeze seven to ten girls into the Tin Lizzy, depending on their age and size. Riding on the running boards was forbidden, otherwise I could have loaded six more with each trip. My dog Skip rode along each trip, sitting on a girl's lap for my protection.

The girl's camp was staffed by a few of the most luscious counselors your eyes ever beheld. My brother Bud and his friend Van (the tenor from *The Pirates of Penzance*) would usually be weekend guests at our cottage. The sight of such a bevy of babes, no longer jail bait, excited Van's ardor which had never ebbed. Actually, from practice, his charm was smoothed to a lustrous polish of perfection. It was only natural that a flashily dressed, tall, handsome gentleman

should be quite attractive to one of the beautiful, overly love-starved counselors. Like a moth is attracted to a flame in the darkness, she did flit.

Such beauty flittering about Van could not go unnoticed. After all, with such an exhilarant, he made the expeditious plans to consummate the lustful seduction of such an eagerly awaiting butterfly. "Don (the Van) Juan" had hidden away a beach blanket in the tall grass in a nearby grove of trees. A blanket is synonymous to sticky flypaper for flittering butterflies — if the grass is wet or dry, no matter which, it works.

Each evening the crowd of young ladies and gentlemen would gather at dusk around benches at the edge of the embankment overlooking the lake to watch the sun go down. "Gentlemen" my butt — each one of us was seething with desire to show each one of these babes that though they were past 18, they had never really been kissed — ONLY BADLY SLOBBERED OVER.

The sun went down into the lake, the clouds glorified the heavenly colors as the afterglow faded into darkness. We snuggled more closely together, singing softly and whispering sweet nothings while communicating with answers of gentle squeezes of the hands and the touch of whispering lips.

Love and romance were all there. Like BUNDLING. Except for the lecherous thoughts held in restraint by our honorable intentions so pledged. The trouble was — the only honor we knew — was two kinds of honor — get on-her and stay on-her. Oh, my aching back, difficult, difficult times.

Good old Van who had been leading the song feast with his dominant, good tenor voice, gradually relinquished his tenor spot to concentrate his attention on the practiced campaign of a seduction over the fragile resistance from his fluttering moth. In the darkness, he arose and oozed out of sight with his prize on one arm and his blanket on the other arm, heading with his prey toward the grove of trees. (It always struck me as quite odd that during football season, a fellow could walk down the street with a steamer blanket on one arm and a girl on the other arm, and no one would think a thing about it).

Skip the dog ever present was quite comfortable leaning against my back, but obviously bored. She too saw Van and his captive butterfly sneaking away from our encampment. Sensing the excitement, Skip followed them. Quiet reigned over this romantic group of would-be or could-be young lovers — bundling and babbling do not mix, so it was damn quiet. The quiet was blasted by a very piercing scream — WOOO — SKIP, GET OUT OF HERE!. The moderate pause followed by a very angry — GET OUT OF HERE!

Shortly after that outburst, Van came storming out of the darkness and in his husky, exaggerated voice of rage, as he pointed a long finger at Skip, he bellowed at me: "IF THAT G.D. DOG CAN'T KEEP HER NOSE OUT OF MY BUSINESS, I'LL SLIT HER THROAT!" You would have to imagine what Skip had done TO BE THREATENED WITH SO VIOLENT AN EXTERMINATION! After all, a cold, wet nose in the wrong place at the wrong time while in the midst of performing the very best technique, can have an instant deflating response. The same kind of deflation that happens when your spouse responds languidly while lying in dignified acquiescence to your most vigorous efforts with this famous quotation, "*DID YOU PAY THE KAUFMANN'S BILL?*"

Of Mice and Men
Down On Sulio's Farm

Summertime on the farms in Salem, Ohio may have hazy days but never lazy days. During threshing days, the only time the workers laid down was for a few minutes after stuffing themselves with food from over-loaded dining tables stretched out in the house and on the lawn under the big oak tree.

One hot hazy day for me at six years of age, I was part of this work force doing the important things like: water boy or "hand me that thing", or pushing the newly threshed grain to the back of the bins in the granary. I too had stuffed myself and stretched out on my belly with all the other men on the cool grass under the big oak tree. That is like luxuriating in that moment of living. Then something flicked past the end of my nose too close for me to identify. I thought it was a grasshopper, but it did not stay on top of the grass. This thing burrowed quickly into the grass. My inquisitive finger went exploring and came out with, *LO AND BEHOLD*, a

Older brother Bud and me.

tiny mouse. It did not struggle when placed in the palm of my hand. It just sat there as still as could be. The mouse looked me over as he kept wiping his tiny nose with little hands on his very short front legs and arms. His hind legs were so long that he had to hop along instead of run like a common mouse. It just sat there on his haunches, observing me and his situation. I extended an investigative index finger to the little fellow, whereupon he climbed on for me to look right into his eyes. I bet he was saying to himself, "Now there is a giant and I don't have a vine for shimmying down.

So, I put the mouse into the breast pocket of my overalls where some kernels of wheat had become lodged as I pulled the wheat to the back of the bins in the granary, as the threshers emptied each box of wheat into the bin. Each box measured a bushel. As each box was filled from the flow of grain pouring out of the threshing machine, it was counted. This way the farmer knew about how many bushels of wheat he was harvesting from one acre.

I thought that in my pocket the mouse would find enough to eat—but the little mouse kept climbing out. So, I put the mouse on top of my head and put my straw hat on real quick before he could hop off. When I wanted to show him off, I just bent way over, head down and shook my head then took my hat off, and there would be my mouse in the hat. Finally, Mrs. Weingart took a look at my mouse. Mrs. Weingart was the mother of Lee, Ethel and Rowland. They and their dad worked that big dairy farm, milking about forty cows morning and night. She told me that I had found a very rare rodent animal known as a *KANGAROO MOUSE.*

At 5 P.M., the whistle at the Mellon Metal Boat Works in Salem sounded off, as it always did at the end of the workday in the mill. When we heard that whistle out there on the farm, it was time to bring in the cows, get the milking done, and wash up for supper. That was when I was supposed to go back to the Suliot farm, where we were spending our vacation. That was about a half-mile walk. But in those days it seemed like miles. If I had not been so hungry, I may have taken a little longer to take a look at a bumblebee nest in the old rail fence by the lane.

The dining room in Suliot's great house was large. It seated twelve guests at the long table and eight at another. Small children always sat with their mothers and all the other old ladies. All the men and older kids ate in a big tent on the side lawn near the kitchen under the big crab apple tree and next to the twelve beehives.

As I dragged myself across the front lawn of the big house, the big dinner bell began to *BONG! BONG!* and Genia Suliot blew on

the big conch shell, *WHOOP! WHOOP!* Those meant come quick, get it while it's *HOT.* Mother spotted me, rushed over, grabbed my hand and dragged me stumbling to the dining room. Not time to clean me up or wash my face. Mother thumped me onto the box on the chair beside her. Others were bustling in, adding to the confusion that occurs just before everything quiets down for the prayer of thanksgiving. Mother seemed quite satisfied until she took another look. I still had my hat on.

Mother said, "Take your hat off!" My head shook from side-to-side. "NO." Mother then spoke in a more demanding voice, and much louder for all to hear, "TAKE YOUR HAT OFF!" My head was still shaking "NO". Mother, intolerant to disobedience, pursed her lips and snatched the hat off my head. There on top of my head sat the little kangaroo mouse exposed for all to see. My little friend made a great leap from my head to the table.

Mother SCREAMED. All the others joined in. Some screamed because they did not know what the others were screaming about. A stampede of stomping feet, upsetting scrapping, banging chairs, erupted in a mad dash to escape to safety, away from that horrible beast I had BRUNG to the table.

After that kangaroo mouse business, I was banished instantly from the big dining room to the tent outside with the men and the big kids. That's where I wanted to be in the first place.

I always knew an elephant was scared of a mouse for fear it might run up its nose, and a woman was scared of a mouse for fear the mouse would run her leg. I know the difference now, but did not learn the fact until years later. I'm quite sure you will not find the explanation on the Internet.

Illustration by Lucy Tuttle Smith

The Cat Attack In The Castle From Which We Sprung

I loved cats. We always had a cat. I was the one who always brought the strays home if they did not arrive on their own. I also had to be stable boss for each one I *BRUNG* home. Cleaning up after a cat until house-broken is a smelly, disgusting chore, which would try the patience of the most ardent feline lover. I had to bathe them too. Pittsburgh was the Smokey City in those days, and cats got dirty fast, and were bathed often no matter if they were black or white. Cats really like being bathed if intro-duced to warm water in the tub when very young kittens. Placing an old cat into a tub of water for the first time is a hazardous experience. They will bite and scratch the heck out of you.

I would teach my cats to jump through a hoop. When the cat sat on a table surrounded by my hands I made a loop with them to make the cat jump over my hands to escape. I repeated this maneuver over and over again, raising my hands higher and higher, and not permitting the cat to escape under my hands. When the cat grew up, it could jump through my arms when I made a hoop while standing up. My cats loved to play stalk. That is, hiding some place and springing out with back up and all fluffed up at your feet if you went tiptoeing about. If I ran from this attack they would give chase. Then they would hide away some place to make

another attack if I continued to tiptoe about.

Sister Helen came home late one night — this time she had a key. Remembering *"DON'T AWAKEN YOUR FATHER,"* Helen tiptoed up the stairs to the second floor, avoiding the squeaky treads. Then along the hallway, as she was tiptoeing to her room, that damn cat sprung out at her feet! Helen's screams awakened Father, Mother and the whole neighborhood.

The House from which we sprung -517 Kelly Ave.,
Wilkinsburg, Pennsylvania.
After the earthquake of 1920 it had a definite tilt.

41

The Threshers Are Coming

Joy at harvest time on the farms is mixed with tension. The anticipation is mixed with worry. The barns are stuffed with shafts of wheat, oats and barley. The fields are dotted with shocks of more grain. Each farm house kitchen is bustling with preparation of food for the gathering of farm families and friends coming for threshing day. Each kitchen plans to deliver the grandest assortment of delicious food the world has ever seen. Prolonged bad wet weather, fires from lightning strikes, and windstorms can be a disaster for the harvest. Prayers are made frequently as eyes scan the clouds. We kids could feel the excitement and responded gleefully, not realizing each farm family helping with our threshing had put their entire year of labor, their entire wealth and their faith in the Lord to answer their prayers for a good harvest.

The threshing machine was a fifty-foot-long red box on four steel wheels. The 20-foot-long-by-18-inch exhaust pipe for blowing off the straw was folded back over the top of the thresher. The thresher was in tow by a steam tractor.

The tractor had giant-sized steel wheels with cleats. The wheels must have been ten feet high. The fire box was aglow with burning coal. The long smokestack belched black smoke. The engineer stood on the backend platform behind the steering wheel. The whistle was loud and shrill. The engineer pulled the whistle cord often as he warned us away from the crunching stones under the great steel wheels. The crunched bits of stone flying from under the wheels were lethal.

After finishing threshing at Weingart's farm in late afternoon, that massive machinery was driven ever so slowly along the dirt road and then up the lane to Suliot's barn.

At Suliot's barn the tractor pushed the thresher backward up the very steep earthen ramp and over the barn bridge onto the floor of the barn. The steam tractor backed down the ramp. Then the men unrolled a long, wide leather-like belt fifty feet long. One end of the belt was slung over the flywheel on the tractor. The other end was lifted over the small pulley on the thresher. The tractor then backed up to take up the slack in the belt. The thresher crew then joined all the men and kids in the dining tent at the side of the big house between the crab apple tree and the beehives.

After dinner the men all gathered to sit on the barn bridge and watch the sun go down. There was a lot of talking and laughing. I just sat there, listening to man talk. My friend Juggie (Julius Suliot, a grandson aged six) was with me, listening. We remembered the men talking about a very large, fat man with the tobacco-stained, bewhiskered, ugly face. His clothes were filthy dirty and he stank something awful. The men always told him to move elsewhere. He ate like a pig in the most slovenly manner. It was disgusting. He ate prodigious quantities of food. The unused portion of the consumption had to be eliminated. To do so, he had to take most of the afternoon to relieve himself of the excess. A problem arose because the privy near the barn had only one hole and it was a big one. The privy was covered all over with grapevine to keep it hidden, shaded and cool. It was situated near to the barn with its back against the apple orchard fence where the pigs were pastured.

The privy had a large drawer to catch the awful. The drawer's back wall was well worn from age and use. Its contents could be recycled easily by dragging the box to a distant field and turned under. Sears and Roebuck catalog pages decorated the spot for a few months thereafter.

The visiting farmers who had come to give a neighborly helping hand with threshing were complaining grievously about this stinking lout's usurpation of the Privy. This gave me an idea how to handle the situation and Juggie agreed with the plan.

We knew that old smelly fatso followed a routine after feasting at noontime. He retired to the one-hole privy near the barn. Sooooo, we rushed back to the privy before he could get there and slid a long plank through the space open at the top of the box at the back of the privy. One end of the plank we centered under the hole in the seat above. The other end stuck out far enough to keep the plank in balance. I climbed up the grapevine to the roof of the privy where I was well out of sight in the leaves. Juggie was to keep watch below and signal to me when the plank was well loaded. We did not wait long. Our victim was right on schedule. Juggie kept a watchful eye upon the loading procedure on the plank as he held his nose. When the load was sufficient to his satisfaction, Juggie gave me the signal. I jumped off the top of the privy to the end of the plank sticking out. There was a spring board effect as I bounced off the plank high into the air simultaneously with the thunderous splat and lion's roar in the privy. It scared the living bagebers out of me. I was running before reaching ground.

We took off through the tall grass in the orchard and around the other side of the barn, across the barnyard and into the silo where we could hide way up at the top window by climbing up through the supports between the inner and outer walls. We stayed up there most of the afternoon until the threshing stopped for the day.

We could hear the men laughing and slapping their thighs. But some times we heard "what otter be done to the backsides of the kids what done that foul deed."

Nobody asked us who done it. Soooo, we never told a lie. We did hear a lot about that poor man who had so little mind left to function with and what an un-christian-like trick it was for any person to do that dastardly trick to another person

There is a lesson to be learned here after one stops laughing. Some people volunteer to cleanup. Would you?

We never saw that stinker after that, the complaining ceased and every one took a bath to make sure he would not become a victim to an un-christian act, you never can tell when. So do what your mother tells you. Take a bath, put on clean underwear, because you never know.

The Suliot farm silo where we hid.
The picture was taken some 85 years after our dastardly deed.

Our Aunt Esther Smith

Aunt Esther, my mother's younger sister by three or four years, was a famous teacher of Latin in Pittsburgh's Peabody High School. As a young woman she had been sent off to Germany for her higher education at a famous university. This was a common custom of old German families. Grandmother Smith's maiden name was Stettner. German had been spoken in her family. So Grandmother Smith spoke German fluently and had always spoken German to Esther.

Grandmother Smith had been born and raised in Columbus, Ohio. Her brother, Herman, stayed in the family home in his ethnic neighborhood. He had raised three children, a boy and two girls. Still the stiff-necked Prussian general, he sent his kids off to Germany to study music. When WWI began he hocked the Kaiser once too often and almost got himself hung. He must have inherited that ramrod stiffness because his great-grandfather had gone AWOL from the German army after he had been shanghaied to sign up for his third hitch in the army. He arrived in Philadelphia and began working on the canal system to the mountains. There he helped drag the canal barges over the mountains to Freeport on the Allegheny River 30 miles north of Pittsburgh. He helped to build keelboats near the point and the old Fort Pitt. From there he floated down the Ohio River to what is now Cincinnati. He then worked the canal that was under construction toward Columbus where he settled down in the local German community and did what most virile men did, he beget so that what he begat could beget etc. Until Willard Stettner arrived to

become a very prominent Presbyterian minister. Well, that is a long way from our dear Esther Smith and the joys we had together.

The lonely years Esther had spent in Germany may have had a profound effect upon her personality. She was a tall woman of sturdy build, round face, black hair, large brown eyes. She must have been the wall-flower of her day. Esther oozed an intellect which intimidated the average man. Also, there were not many men left to pick from after the Spanish-American War and WWI. Soooo, Aunt Esther remained single. She concentrated on teaching and working with Governor Pinchot to establish a pension plan for teachers long before there was a teacher's union. Miss Smith never had a problem with discipline in her classroom. When that big round face began to swell up and turn red, those big brown eyes would bulge out and rivet the culprit stiff. No Prussian General could have done it better.

For years Esther commuted from Wilkinsburg's 1312 Wood Street to Peabody High School in East Liberty, riding on the Hamilton Avenue streetcar. She finally nerved herself up to buy the first Model T Ford Coupe. The one with glass windows that slid up and down on a strap in a slit in the door and side. It had one door.

Esther was very proud of this Tin Lizzy, and to prove it, she sat bolt upright behind the wheel. Being a large woman, there was little space left to maneuver. Aunt Esther was always invited to spend some summer vacation time with us. Now with this new car, she decided to drive the 120 miles to our cottage on the shore of Lake Erie.

Dad had rented one of Captain Carrol's four cottages on the edge of the high banks overlooking Lake Erie, three miles from Conneaut, Ohio.

The roads in those days were winding like cow paths over the countryside. A few miles were black topped (thanks to Pinchot). Many miles of road were mud, some were gravel surfaced and washboarded like Route 7 north in Ohio.

Aunt Esther prepared herself well for this safari into the unknown with great diligence. Since road signs were few and far between, Esther obtained a compass. As it turned out, her sense of direction was more reliable than the compass, especially when she disregarded the compass reading inside her Tin Can. She did have a road map of scanty information. Esther packed herself a lunch big enough for a cross-country tour. When her car was fully loaded she took off. This takeoff can not be compared with that of a 747 except for the noises inside that rattletrap. The whole darn thing had built-in things that made it rattle constantly. The intensity of the rattle would turn to a high pitch depending upon the speed and the bumps in the road. The crankshaft was not balanced, so as the revolutions of the engine increased for speed, the buzzing sound of the vibrations mixed in with the rattles would increase the decibels created by a swarm of bees. Esther really buzzed the fields as she whizzed by.

Esther's odyssey began at dawn because she did not want to be lost on the roads at night. She was physically fit and well watered from both ends before she departed —since comfort stations were far apart or non-existent and that time of year the corn in the fields was only knee high. No doubt she had put on her clean underwear because "you can never tell."

Esther made very good time in spite of a stop for a snack before reaching Butler. Then there was Mercer and then Greenville and Jamestown for a snack. Finally, as the sun was setting into Lake Erie she arrived in one piece, all covered with dust. The remains of her picnic she presented to us as a dainty morsel – half an apple, half an orange, half a banana, half a ham sandwich and a few crumbs of chocolate cake. Every year thereafter, dear Aunt Esther upon her arrival would present us with her DAINTY MORSELS. We received her as a conquering hero. Caesar could not have been more pleased. We also noted that Esther seemed to continue to shake all over for an hour or two after dismounting from her wheels.

After two years the model "T" coupe had rattled itself to pieces. Aunt Esther purchased a brand-new six-cylinder two-door Essex sedan. It was a long, slick low under-slung all-black beauty with enough room under the steering wheel for Esther's long legs and portly torso. The Essex had become a popular low-priced car when Henry Ford closed down his plants to retool for the Model A car. Aunt Esther was quite happy with her new car. It had a smooth ride, it did not vibrate or rattle and it would speed along at 40 mph over the washboard gravel roads without shaking itself apart as the Tin Lizzy did.

Three years later, while Aunt Esther was spending a week or two with the family at the cottage, her Essex had become a little shabby. She talked to us fellows about painting her car. Brother Bud and I each had a friend spending a few days with us. We talked it over and decided that we could do the job. Since the painting would be done in the open field next to the cottage and the weather report indicated no rain for several days, preparation began immediately. We rushed to the hardware store in

Conneaut to get four paintbrushes and a gallon of black enamel. We rushed back to Esther's Essex and began slopping on the enamel. I mentioned slopping it on because the enamel was so thick and sticky that we pressed the gluey stuff on instead of sweeping it on with brush strokes. With four of us smearing on the enamel we were finished in jig time. What we had created was a sparkling black diamond. All the neighbors came to view the masterpiece. Aunt Esther was thrilled with the new look. We fellows were proud of the job well done.

That is when we all noticed a large black cloud coming toward us way out north over Lake Erie. Rain had not been in the forecast. Soooo, we were not concerned. However that black cloud kept approaching and before we realized what the black cloud really was, we were in for it. A swirling mass of Canadian Soldiers, insects with gossamer wings spreading three inches on mosquito-like bodies. They settled in mass over the fields, trees and roads. On the screens of the porches they matted so thick the sunlight was shut out.

When the invasion ceased we found dear Aunt Esther's Essex covered all over with a mass of fluttering wings of Canadian Soldiers stuck firmly to that sticky enamel. As the breezes waft over the wings they waved like wheat in the fields. Some folks thought the car had a fur coat. We tried to pick the buggers off the sticky black enamel without success. In fact that picking business made our Van Goo Goo all prickly. We decided to let nature take its course. Let the wind blow off the gossamer wings as the enamel dried. The imprint of the desiccated bodies remained over the finish to give it a stippled appearance as well as a very interesting conversation piece if mixed with a lot of BS as is so often done to describe an impressionist's rendition.

Aunt Esther took the result of the paint job in stride. Being a great optimist, she declared that she could not have done it cheaper and that the enamel was so thick over the metal and so sticky, the Essex would last forever.

When the paint job was completely dry we could not get into the damn car! We found the doors to be glued tight shut. We spent hours teasing the doors open. Then, Aunt Esther got into the act, she put a big fist around the door handle and with the full weight of her big behind behind her, she gave a mighty pull. The cracking sound of the enamel releasing could be heard for miles around.

Preparations for Esther's return to school began 24 hours before departure. The lunch basket was securely packed with ample provisions for a non-stop transcontinental trek. Her bags were strapped securely to the top of the Essex. Each bag had the usual going-away gift, a nice large flat stone from the beach in each suitcase. The girls gave Aunt Esther a *DAINTY MORSEL* snack from the lunch table neatly wrapped. It contained the chicken carcass with feet. We knew that she had done what her mother had always told her to do that day. Her underwear was not on the line – she had the clean pair on. After she was comfortably seated behind the wheel, one of the boys hung a large sign on the back of her car: "*MY ESSEX, HOW'S YOURS*".

Aunt Esther told us that she had had a most joyous ride all the way to *HIGH BODY PEA SCHOOL*. Every body seemed to pass her on the road smiling and waving to her. She had parked on the street near the school that day and had not noticed the sign on the back end of the car. However, after school, half the student body and the teaching staff were congregated around her Essex to tell her that their own felt just fine.

The Chicken At 517 Kelly

At Easter time the newly hatched peeps, ducks and sometimes rabbits would be for sale as gifts for children. The Animal Rights League did away with that joy of ownership of a pet forever. Before A.R.L., I managed to get two yellow peeps for my two-year-old nephew, Chum. He lived with his mother and his dad, Bill, in a second-floor duplex along Celeron Street a few city blocks away from 517 Kelly.

In four or five weeks, one chick had finally expired. The second chick had grown considerably. Bill and Helen decided to take the chick back to 517. The chicken could not be potty trained. By that time, that chick was going to be a rooster, who thought he was people. Chicks do that, you know. There he had the freedom of the front and back yards, and sometimes the kitchen if he was lucky enough to miss the swinging screen door.

Well, it was not long before he was part of the family. Each morning, he would fly to the highest pole of the backyard fence near the alley. There he would crow like a real barnyard cock, disturbing the sleep of our dear suffering neighbors. Dad was very fond of this bird. He fed that bird scraps from his breakfast every morning as he set off to catch the train to town. The bird followed him down the alley to Hay then up Hay to Rebecca across from the Clutton's Drug store in the Colonial Building. There the rooster bid good-bye and returned to the backyard at 517 to pursue whatever it is that chickens do. Dad took a lot of ribbing from his fellow commuters because each evening that crazy chicken met Dad at the corner and together they would walk down the alley to 517's backyard. In the kitchen, Dad would give Mother a peck on each cheek. Then he would return to the backyard, and set himself down on his old wicker chair with the fat reed arms to read the evening paper.

The bird would hop to Dad's lap, then to the arm of the chair, then to Dad's shoulder, where he would stretch his neck out and around to look into Dad's eye through the lens of Dad's *pince-nez* spectacles. This was not an eyeball-to-eyeball confrontation. That crazy bird just loved to see himself reflected from the glass. A real mirror image of his face. He just knew that there was another chicken in there someplace.

One thing I learned about what chickens do, when the things chickens do are not supervised, was happening all too often. Reports were circulating that there was an ATTACK CHICKEN in the neighborhood.

Since we were the proud owners of the only chicken in that part of town, I thought the accusations should be investigated to justify the veracity of those reports. Dutifully I planked my backside on our front porch steps to observe the scene. A privet hedge surrounded our small patch of green lawn and lined the flag stone sidewalk in the front. A large maple tree at the curb shaded it all. Double streetcar tracks ran down the center of the street, and on the other side of the street, a motorcycle policeman had pulled up and parked. He seemed to be observing the full length of the street. Except for an occasional streetcar banging along, we had a very quiet community.

The bird had found a cool comfortable dust bowl under the privet hedge in the shade of the maple tree. I did not see him there until a nicely dressed housewife came mincing down the sidewalk with her arms full of packages. When she reached our front walk that damn chicken attacked that poor woman's feet. With feathers all fluffed out, he pecked and cackled around her feet like a cock-a-demon. Blood-curdling screams exploded form the victim as she took flight down the sidewalk to Pitt Street, where she imploded onto a bench.

I thought the damned rooster had put on a very amusing performance—obviously, the victim in full flight down the street was of another opinion.

The policeman across the street damn near fell off his bike. He came across the street to me, laughing with tears on his cheeks. When he finally composed himself enough to give me an authoritarian official notice, he finally said, "The Chief has had so many complaints about an attack chicken, that he had decided the attacks must be investigated." Then the policeman said, "I have never had so much fun reporting and officially handling a complaint. You must do something about that damn chicken of yours."

Soo, we gave that damn chicken to dear old Mrs. Olson. She knew what to do with him. She ate him! Our family mourned his passing.

The front porch of 517 Kelly from which I observed the escapades of the attack chicken

One Summer Time
(It Weren't No Dream)

We survived without sulfa drug, penicillin, polio vaccine, and without airconditioning at 517 Kelly Street. Summertime could be an ordeal for all us poor critters. That is just the way it was, so make the best of it. Mother had ordered Bud and me to move our brass beds from the third-floor back room to the second-floor front room and place the head end of the beds against the front windows. That was a great relief from the insufferable hot air of the third-floor summertime heat. Sleeping in shorts with a sheet to pull over us if needed was a welcome relief.

Times were tough in the early '30s. The depression was deepening. No summertime jobs for young bucks were to be had. Dad had not lost a cent in the stock market because he never had any in the market in the first place. Brother Bud and his friend Van were selling telephones on commission at 25 cents for each phone sold. Their territory was in SOHO, the most depressed area in the city. No one in SOHO had 25 cents. One day, they sold one, then walked into town on Forbes Street, to Dad's office in the Keystone Building on 4th Avenue. Dad was still in his office. That is when they found out that they had only 25 cents for the three of them. The 25 cents bought three streetcar tokens for their ride home to Wilkinsburg. *(TALK ABOUT INFLATION!)*

I had taken the day off from painting the house to visit my college sweetheart, Flora Dale in little Washington, 30-some miles south of Pittsburgh. My father's distant relative, who was passing through town, had been invited to stay the night at our home.

Since I would not be expected to return home that night, my bed would be empty. Therefore, it would be no additional trouble for Mother.

I had planned to spend the night at my fraternity house. My sweetheart had sent me packing at midnight. So, I went to the fraternity house to find it had just closed at the end of summer school. I had to drive back home that night through dense fog and smog. That was 30 miles of torture on a road which had been made over a cow path. I arrived at 517 Kelly about 3 A.M., without a key to the house. *"DON'T AWAKEN YOUR FATHER"* was still recorded in my memory. So, over the porch roof I climbed and started to climb through my window at the head of my bed. A MIGHTY ROAR from within put me into reverse suddenly to the right, just as a mighty fist and arm came out the window and a bent rod of brass bed whizzed past me!

The uproar following that commotion had Bud, Dad, and Mother bursting with laughter and the neighborhood hollering for quiet. Had that fist ever connected with me, I would have landed 20 feet down on the front lawn.

The Iceman Cometh

My older brother was three years ahead of me. We did have some sibling rivalry at times, but never over serious things. He was a great innovator of new and wonderful ideas for doing things to earn a buck or trade a toy for a pair of bantam chickens. He would try anything. I loved and admired how he managed to get things done with all the odds against him. I always wanted to do the things he did until he became a fan of Charley Chaplin. He was a miniature of the great comedian in action. Thank heavens we did not have talking movies in those days, or Bud would have mimicked Charley's voice, too. The sound we had in the nickelodeon was from what we kids made and the pianist could pound out of that old upright piano under the screen. Brother Bud ate as Charley did, he waddled when he walked with his feet turned out as Charley did and always made his corners on the outside foot with the inside leg held out at a right angle to keep his balance almost falling over just as Charley did. He had practiced all these mannerisms so intensely that he had become canalized. Bud could not stop living Charley Chaplin. Our father would become exasperated with Bud's shenanigans every Sunday morning on the way to church as Bud would make every corner on one foot just as Charley did. I remember Bud doing that little Charley footwork as he rushed to church on his wedding day.

High school days finally arrived. In those days Red Grange was the talk of the sports world. Every kid who wanted to play football wanted to be as good as Red Grange. Well, Bud was not big enough to play football, but he did get into the locker room as a reporter for the local newspaper. He caught the Red Grange fever there. It must have been a very severe case because he found out that Red Grange had delivered ice in the summer time. He got himself a job delivering ice from the ice plant in Edgewood, our neighboring suburb. His route would cover our area in Wilkinsburg.

Bud's 125 pounds was never meant for that kind of labor but he showed up bright and early that first day after school closed for the summer. The ice wagon had been backed into the loading dock in front of the shoot from which 300 pounds of ice came thundering out and slid into that old ice wagon. When it was loaded Bud hooked a chain across the back to keep the load from sliding out. He climbed into the driver's seat. Then he asked the boss, "Which route do I take?" The boss said, "Follow the horse." After that, all Bud had to do was watch for the ice card hung in a window to see how many pounds of ice were needed in the customer's icebox. Old Dobin, the horse, seemed to keep an eye open for those cards too because he seemed to stop automatically if Bud should happen to miss one.

Most of the ice was delivered to the customers in a very large apartment complex fronting Hay St. between Rebecca and Franklin Streets, the Colonial Building and the Colonial Annex. These buildings had good thick walls of brick but were all wood inside. Each building was four stories high. Each apartment had a good-sized living room, dining room, kitchen, bathroom and two bedrooms. Thirty or more of these units were occupied most of the time and most of them had ice cards displayed. Bud, the indomitable ice man, serviced those units all summer long, lugging 25- to 50-pound chunks of ice up the stairs to his customers.

He had to collect cash from each of his customers and could not trade his services for the yearnings of a few oversexed house fraus and widows who propositioned him. Anyway, he was too honorable and had to save his strength.

Modern science finally developed the electric refrigerator and did away with the iceman's job. He stashed away a few hard-earned bucks to begin his education at the University of Pittsburgh. He also found his place in the newspaper business as a reporter, advertising and salesmanship.

Printed in the United States
by Baker & Taylor Publisher Services